ANIMALS OF MASS DESTRUCTION

LOCUSTS

Gareth Stevens
PUBLISHING

By Caitlin McAneney

Please visit our website, www.garethstevens.com. For a free color catalog of all our high-quality books, call toll free 1-800-542-2595 or fax 1-877-542-2596.

Library of Congress Cataloging-in-Publication Data

McAneney, Caitlin.
Locusts / by Caitlin McAneney.
 p. cm. — (Animals of mass destruction)
Includes index.
ISBN 978-1-4824-1052-5 (pbk.)
ISBN 978-1-4824-1053-2 (6-pack)
ISBN 978-1-4824-1051-8 (library binding)
1. Locusts — Juvenile literature. I. McAneney, Caitlin. II. Title.
QL508.A2 M33 2015
595.7—d23

First Edition

Published in 2015 by
Gareth Stevens Publishing
111 East 14th Street, Suite 349
New York, NY 10003

Copyright © 2015 Gareth Stevens Publishing

Designer: Andrea Davison-Bartolotta
Editor: Therese Shea

Photo credits: Cover, p. 1 (main) Denny Allen/Gallo Images/Getty Images; cover, p. 1 (inset) iStock/Thinkstock; series art (all textured backgrounds, yellow striped line) Elisanth/Shutterstock.com; series art (caption boxes) Fatseyeva/Shutterstock.com; series art (orange boxes) Tracie Andrews/Shutterstock.com; pp. 4–5 Marek R. Swadzba/Shutterstock.com; p. 6 Guenter Fischer/Getty Images; pp. 6–7, 16–17, 20–21, 24–25 Gianni Tortoli/Photo Researchers/Getty Images; pp. 8–9, 10 Ruvan Boshoff/iStock/Thinkstock; pp. 10–11 Patipas/iStock/Thinkstock; p. 12 Nigel Cattlin/Visuals Unlimited/Getty Images; pp. 12–13 ©iStockphoto.com/ZippyZoo; p. 14 Dorling Kindersley/Getty Images; pp. 14–15 PRILL/Shutterstock.com; p. 16 (both) Mirek Kijewski/Shutterstock.com; pp. 18–19 Superstock/Getty Images; pp. 22–23 © iStockphoto.com/thad; p. 23 (inset) David Steele/Shutterstock.com; p. 24 German School/The Bridgeman Art Library/Getty Images; p. 25 (inset) Jacoby's Art Gallery/Wikimedia Commons; p. 26 Joel Sartore/National Geographic/Getty Images; pp. 26–27 Maksymowicz/iStock/Thinkstock; p. 28 arka38/Shutterstock.com; pp. 28–29 Uriel Sinai/Getty Images.

Printed in the United States of America

CPSIA compliance information: Batch #CS15GS: For further information contact Gareth Stevens, New York, New York at 1-800-542-2595.

CONTENTS

Words in the glossary appear in **bold** type the first time they are used in the text.

WHAT ARE LOCUSTS?

You've probably heard of grasshoppers, but do you know about locusts? Grasshoppers, crickets, katydids, and locusts are part of the animal group Orthoptera. These insects have wings and **antennae**, are good jumpers, and rub body parts together to make sounds.

Unlike most of its relatives, the locust is a very **destructive** insect. Swarms, or huge groups of locusts, do great harm to crops. For thousands of years, a swarm of locusts has been known as a plague, a word that means a large number of harmful creatures or an event that causes great suffering or loss. Both meanings apply to locusts.

Chew On This!

"Orthoptera" means "straight wings." Locust wings are very flexible, or bendable, which helps them fly.

Locusts communicate by rubbing their back legs and wings together to make sounds. Younger locusts, like this one, don't have fully grown wings yet.

AROUND THE WORLD

There are about a dozen **species** of locusts. They can be found everywhere except in very cold places like Antarctica.

Different species live in different parts of the world. For example, the desert locust can be found in Africa, the Middle East, and Asia. The Australian plague locust lives in Australia, while the American locust lives in the United States, Mexico, and Central America. The migratory locust covers the most area. It lives in Africa, Asia, Australia, New Zealand, and sometimes Europe.

Chew On This!

Locusts have four wings. There are two smaller wings on top, and two larger back wings that fold out when they fly.

The brown locust is a pest to southern Africa, while the desert locust (shown here) causes trouble in North Africa.

7

ACTING THE PART

Many people mistake locusts for grasshoppers. They both have two pairs of wings, a three-part body, and long back legs. However, locusts' **behavior** sets them apart. Locusts sometimes live alone, while grasshoppers always do. But when it rains and green plants grow, locust numbers increase. Then, they start to crowd together. Scientists call this the "gregarious **phase**." "Gregarious" means being social and friendly.

In this phase, locusts **breed** and feed on whatever they can find. Their wings and bodies grow bigger. Some species even change color.

common milkweed locust

Not all locusts go through the gregarious phase. That happens only to those that live during swarming conditions—enough rain, warmth, and green plants.

9

MIGRATION

Migration is another part of the locust's behavior. That means they move from one place to another in search of food. Once the locusts breed, their growing swarm needs to be fed. With larger wings, thanks to the gregarious phase, these locusts are ready to migrate.

Locusts can fly hundreds of miles in a swarm over a few days. Many take off at night and ride strong winds. Migrating swarms can be made of **trillions** of locusts.

Chew On This!

In 1869, desert locusts migrated all the way from west Africa to England. That's more than 3,000 miles (4,828 km)!

While many fly a few feet above the ground, some locusts have been known to fly more than 3,000 feet (914 m) high.

A LOCUST'S LIFE

Female locusts drill into the soil with a body part called an ovipositor. Then, they lay a pod of 30 or more eggs and cover it with a liquid for protection. During the gregarious phase, many females lay their eggs at the same time. This means there will be many more locusts. Unhatched locusts grow faster in warmer, wetter weather.

Nymphs (NIHMFS) hatch from the locust eggs. They look like adult locusts, but they don't have wings yet.

locust nymph

During the gregarious phase, egg beds—or areas where locusts lay eggs—are very crowded because many females are laying their eggs in the same place.

WHAT'S NEXT?

Nymphs can't fly, but they can hop. They go through growth phases called instars. After each instar, nymphs lose, or shed, their exoskeleton, which is a shell-like skin. This is called molting. They begin to grow wings and become more like adult locusts.

There are usually five instars in a locust's life, and they happen faster in swarming conditions. After the last molt, locusts have their adult wings. They're soon able to breed, too.

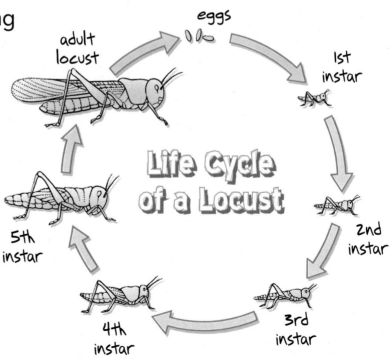

Life Cycle of a Locust

eggs

1st instar

2nd instar

3rd instar

4th instar

5th instar

adult locust

Because they can't fly yet, locust nymphs are called hoppers. They often form large groups that travel close to the ground.

Chew On This!

Even after the final instar, the young locust can't fly. Its wings need a few more days to harden. Locusts are called fledglings at this point.

15

BIG EATERS

How do such small animals cause so much trouble? Locusts are big eaters. A locust can eat as much as it weighs every day. The bigger the swarm, the more crops the locusts destroy.

How big is a swarm? Some swarms can cover over 460 square miles (1,191 sq km). There may be trillions of locusts, and each one is hungry. A swarm of locusts that size can eat over 400 million pounds (182 million kg) in just a single day!

Locusts will often eat any crop in their path. That's a lot of valuable food for people.

17

LOCUSTS IN ANCIENT TIMES

Locust swarms have always been a problem for people. Ancient writings describe people going hungry from locust swarms eating crops and food supplies, especially in North Africa. The Bible contains a famous story of a plague of locusts eating Egyptian crops. People believed they were sent by God as a punishment.

Ancient Greek and Roman writings also tell of locusts and their terrible effects on communities. One writer described a swarm so thick it blocked the light of the sun!

Chew On This!

Some scientists believe a huge locust swarm flew from Africa to America between 3 and 5 million years ago.

Artwork and writings about locusts show how people felt about them in the past.

DESERT DISASTER

Some parts of the world still suffer greatly from locusts. Today, northern and western Africa, the Middle East, and western Asia are perhaps the hardest hit. Many small countries in these areas depend heavily on their crops. Some countries don't have the supplies to fight swarms.

A locust swarm can leave countries without food or money. In 1986, a locust plague hit 23 African countries, including Sudan and Ethiopia, and remained until 1989. Millions of people suffered from hunger because the locusts ate their crops.

Chew On This!

In 1958, locust swarms in Ethiopia ate enough food to feed about a million people for a whole year.

Ethiopia is an African country that has long suffered locust plagues. Here, people run for cover from a swarm of locusts.

21

TROUBLE DOWN UNDER!

Australia is home to three main kinds of locusts. While the migratory locust and spur-throated locust cause problems, the worst pest is the Australian plague locust. Australian plague locust **outbreaks** happen often and can cover a lot of land. Swarms have been reported since the 1870s and can last more than a year.

Luckily, Australia has an effective system of locust control, which involves **pesticide** use. A 1984 outbreak cost Australia about $5 million in crops. Without locust control actions, Australia might have lost over $100 million!

Locusts don't damage only crops, but also valuable pasture where livestock eat.

ROCKY MOUNTAIN NIGHTMARE

While locusts are huge pests in other parts of the world, the biggest locust outbreak was actually in North America! In 1875, Rocky Mountain locusts formed the largest swarm that's ever been recorded. The swarm covered an area about 1,800 miles (2,897 km) long and 110 miles (177 km) wide.

The locusts were everywhere, eating any plants they could find, and settlers didn't have the tools to fight them. Farmers in the American Midwest called 1875 the "Year of the Locust."

Laura Ingalls Wilder wrote a famous book called *On the Banks of Plum Creek*. In it, she described how locusts destroyed her Minnesota farm during the locust swarm of 1875.

Rocky Mountain locusts

Chew On This!

Dr. Albert Child reported on the Rocky Mountain locust swarm, so it's sometimes called "Albert's swarm." He believed the swarm contained about 3.5 trillion locusts.

EXTINCT!

If there were trillions of Rocky Mountain locusts in North America, where are they now? Why don't plagues of locusts destroy Midwest crops anymore? That's a mystery scientists have been trying to answer.

The last Rocky Mountain locust was found in 1902. Since then, they've become **extinct**. Scientists think the likely reason is that settlers plowed soil to get it ready for farming and dug up locust egg beds. Today, Midwestern farms are some of the most successful in the world.

Rocky Mountain locust

The answer to the Rocky Mountain locust mystery is important, because it could teach us how to control locust swarms in other countries.

PEST CONTROL

How can we control locust outbreaks? This is an important question. Many African and Middle Eastern countries can't afford to lose their crops.

Today, the Food and Agriculture Organization (FAO) of the **United Nations** works to warn countries of possible outbreaks before they happen. They also control locust outbreaks using pesticides. Unfortunately, pesticides can be harmful to nature and people. As science advances, there's hope we can fight this destructive pest more naturally.

This plane is spraying pesticides over Israel in March 2013 in an attempt to control a destructive locust outbreak.

GLOSSARY

antenna: a feeler on the head of some animals. The plural of "antenna" is "antennae."

behavior: the way an animal acts

breed: to come together to make babies

destructive: causing harm

extinct: no longer living

outbreak: a sudden occurrence of something unpleasant or dangerous

pesticide: something used to kill pests, such as bugs

phase: a stage in a process or sequence of events

species: a group of living things that are all the same kind

trillion: one thousand billion, or 1,000,000,000,000

United Nations: a group of nations that united after World War II for the purpose of working together to solve problems more peacefully

FOR MORE INFORMATION

Books

Jackson, Cari. *Bugs That Destroy.* New York, NY: Marshall Cavendish Benchmark, 2009.

Kravetz, Jonathan. *Locusts.* New York, NY: PowerKids Press, 2006.

Websites

ABC Learn: Locusts
abceducation.net.au/videolibrary/view/locusts-109
This video takes a look at the destructive nature of the Australian plague locust. Watch real footage of locust swarms!

Facts for Kids on Locusts
animals.pawnation.com/kids-locusts-8949.html
Read more about locusts and why people fear them.

Locust
animals.nationalgeographic.com/animals/bugs/locust/
Find out more about locusts and other animals on this website.

INDEX